RETURN OF THE JEDI

MISSION 3

WRITTEN BY STEVE SAVILE

HENDERSON
PUBLISHING LTD

TM & © 1997 Lucasfilm Ltd.
All rights reserved.
Used under authorization.

The harsh landscape of Tatooine stretched from horizon to horizon. Twin suns beat down relentlessly on the desert. Two figures made their way towards the gates of the mighty sandstone palace of Jabba the Hutt.
"Of course I'm worried," C-3PO fussed. "And you should be too. Lando Calrissian and poor Chewbacca never returned from this awful place."
R2-D2 chirped defiantly in answer.
"Don't be so sure. If I told you half the things I have heard about Jabba the Hutt you'd probably short-circuit. Are you sure this is the right place?"
Artoo chirped again.
"Better knock, I suppose," Threepio said uncertainly, reaching out to tap on the massive iron doors. "...Well, there doesn't seem to be anyone in. Let's go back and tell Master Luke..."
Even as he spoke, a strange mechanical eye popped out of the door to stare at them.

"I don't think they are going to let us in, Artoo." Threepio turned his back, but the huge iron door groaned and began to rise. Without waiting, Artoo wheeled through. "Artoo, Artoo...we shouldn't rush into this... Let's just deliver Master Luke's message and get out of here..." But Artoo was away, leaving Threepio to chase after him.

INSIDE JABBA'S PALACE
Hidden within the grid are twelve characters (plus one secret bonus) – can you find them all?

D	R	A	U	G	N	A	E	R	R	O	M	A	G
F	G	V	B	R	J	N	H	I	K	D	L	H	D
Z	A	B	Q	F	U	U	U	R	M	N	Y	V	T
C	G	L	W	E	H	T	S	D	F	A	D	R	H
H	U	K	U	T	A	R	T	O	O	L	O	S	G
E	N	B	D	B	N	O	A	Q	A	C	I	A	I
W	A	D	B	A	S	F	R	S	N	O	P	O	N
B	Q	A	D	W	O	B	L	A	W	C	E	E	K
A	J	P	G	A	L	I	R	L	Q	H	E	E	I
C	S	D	L	R	O	B	A	I	J	V	R	M	D
C	O	K	E	S	M	L	U	K	E	Y	H	I	E
A	L	E	I	Q	Y	M	N	G	D	V	T	J	J
S	A	L	A	C	I	O	U	S	C	R	U	M	B
R	A	N	C	W	G	Y	Y	N	I	H	G	G	O

LUKE; LEIA; HAN SOLO; CHEWBACCA; ARTOO; THREEPIO; LANDO; JABBA; RANCOR; SALACIOUS CRUMB; BIB FORTUNA; GAMORREAN GUARD

RETURN OF THE JEDI

nside Jabba's palace, strange creatures gathered around the slug-like gangster on his throne.

"The message, Artoo…" Threepio shuffled uncomfortably beneath Jabba's stare.

Artoo whirred, swivelling to beam a shimmering blue hologram of Luke Skywalker into the room. "Greetings Exalted One," the hologram began. "I am Luke Skywalker, Jedi Knight and friend to Captain Solo. I seek an audience to bargain for Solo's life." Jabba's court of villains roared with laughter. "With your wisdom I am sure that we can work out an arrangement…as a token of my goodwill I present to you a gift – these two droids."

"What did he say? This can't be…" Threepio whined. "Artoo, you're playing the wrong message!"
"There will be no bargain," Jabba rasped, waving at his favourite decoration. Encased in carbonite, Han Solo hung from the wall in a dimly lit alcove.
"We're doomed," Threepio moaned pitifully.

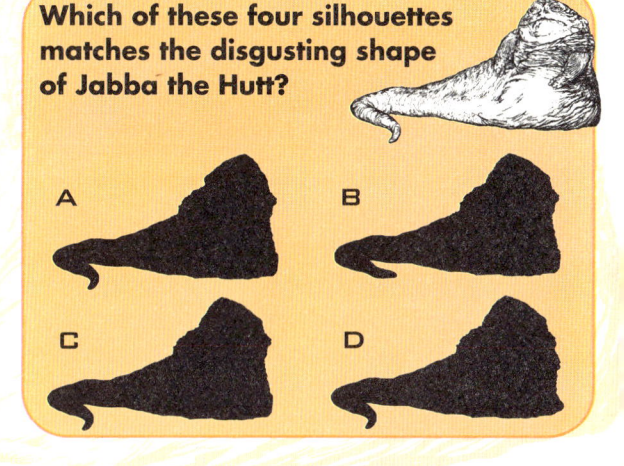

Which of these four silhouettes matches the disgusting shape of Jabba the Hutt?

A

B

C

D

RETURN OF THE JEDI

The gangster's court buzzed with music. In the centre of the floor a dancer twirled and span. Jabba watched through the smoke. He gestured for the dancer to sit by his feet. Instead, she backed up, shaking fearfully. Jabba grunted and hit a switch. Suddenly the floor was gone from beneath her feet.

Her screams were drowned by the rumbling roar of the beast in the pit. Some of the drinkers crowded around to watch the dancer's sudden death. Jabba simply laughed – an evil, slobbering sound which died in the gangster's throat as a steel-masked bounty hunter pushed his way through the crowd with his chained prize.

The bounty hunter bowed low. "I have come for the bounty on this Wookiee."

"At last we have the mighty Chewbacca! The reward is twenty-five thousand."

"Fifty thousand, no less." The bounty hunter primed the thermal detonator in his hand, lifting it so all could see it. Blasters levelled on him. The bounty hunter waited. The detonator ticked…

"This bounty hunter is my kind of scum," Jabba joked finally. "Thirty-five thousand. No more." The bounty hunter tilted his head. He had spotted Lando Calrissian in the crowd, disguised as one of Jabba's skiff guards.
The bounty hunter disarmed the thermal detonator.

How many times can you find the name Jabba in this grid?

J	A	B	J	A	J	A
A	J	A	A	J	B	A
A	B	A	B	A	J	J
B	J	A	B	A	A	B
A	J	J	A	B	B	A
B	A	J	B	B	A	J
A	B	B	A	J	B	A

RETURN OF THE JEDI 7

The throne room was dark and empty. The party was over. Night filtered in. The bounty hunter crept down the stairs, moving slowly to the carbonite coffin hanging in the alcove. He didn't make a sound.

Set in to the side of the slab were the controls to activate the decarbonisation process. The bounty hunter studied them for a moment, making sense of the curious symbols.

Which shape is next in the sequence?

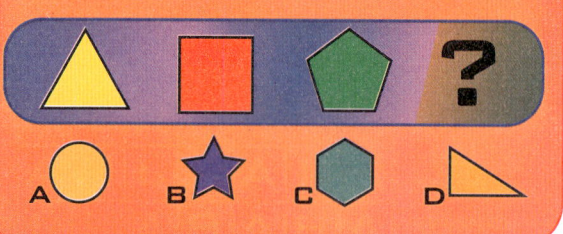

The bounty hunter pressed the final shape, beginning the thawing process. Solo's encased body began to glow red as the metal started to melt away from his skin. Pinpoints of light grew into holes, and then suddenly Han's body slumped free, landing in a heap on the floor and lying still.

RETURN OF THE JEDI

The bounty hunter leaned in close, checking Han was still alive, then pulled him in to a sitting position. "Just relax for a moment." The bounty hunter's voice sounded ugly and metallic through his helmet. Han shivered in his arms, and touched his fingers to his eyes.

"I can't see."

"Hibernation sickness. Your eyesight will return."

"Where am I?"

"Jabba's palace."

Han reached out a hand blindly, feeling the steel helmet, fearful that Boba Fett had come to finish him off. "Who are you?"

The bounty hunter removed his helmet, revealing Princess Leia Organa. "Someone who loves you," she whispered.

Deep, rumbling laughter filled the room. A curtain slid back. There sat Bib Fortuna, Boba Fett, several guards and Jabba himself.

"I know that laugh," Han said. "Hey Jabba, I was just on my way to pay you back, but I got a little side-tracked. It's not my fault…"
"It's too late for that, Solo. Take him away." Guards grabbed Han.
"Look Jabba, I'll pay you triple, you're throwing away a fortune here. Don't be a fool!"
Leia stared desperately after Han. "We have powerful friends…you're going to regret this…"
"I'm sure," Jabba slobbered.

The name Skywalker appears in this grid only once. Can you find the full name?

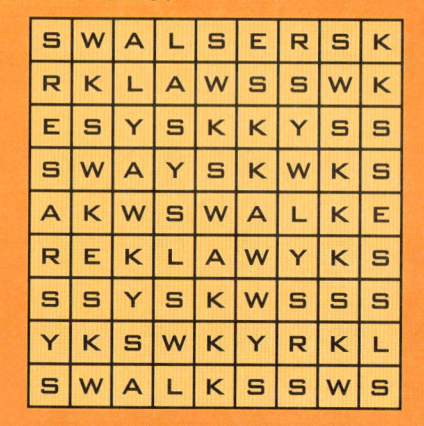

S	W	A	L	S	E	R	S	K
R	K	L	A	W	S	S	W	K
E	S	Y	S	K	K	Y	S	S
S	W	A	Y	S	K	W	K	S
A	K	W	S	W	A	L	K	E
R	E	K	L	A	W	Y	K	S
S	S	Y	S	K	W	S	S	S
Y	K	S	W	K	Y	R	K	L
S	W	A	L	K	S	S	W	S

RETURN OF THE JEDI

The huge iron gate of Jabba's palace groaned open, spilling light into the cavernous complex. A hooded figure stood in the gateway, clad in the robes of a Jedi Knight.

Luke Skywalker had travelled a long way, yet here he was back on Tatooine. He was a man now, not a young farmboy. He had learned much and lost a lot.

Here he was, without blaster or lightsaber, ready to rescue his friend Han Solo. He stood for a while, absorbing the atmosphere of Jabba's vile den. Stepping through the archway, two Gamorrean guards crossed their weapons to block his path. Gently, he raised a hand to touch each of the weapons, and before they could fight back the guards fell away, clutching at their throats. Luke lowered his hand, letting them breathe again, and walked on.

Jabba's lieutenant, Bib Fortuna, waited around the next corner. "You must be Skywalker," Bib said quickly, wagging a finger.

RETURN OF THE JEDI

"I must speak with Jabba," Luke said softly. "No, no. The great Jabba is asleep," Bib protested. Luke didn't break his stride. He looked deep into Bib's eyes, and made a slight gesture with his finger. "You will take me to Jabba now."

Bib shook his head slightly…what were his orders? Oh yes. "I will take you to see Jabba now," he echoed Luke's words. As they approached Jabba's throne, Luke saw Leia sitting there, by Jabba's gluttonous belly. She was held by a chain and dressed like a dancing girl. Bib introduced Luke to his master, startling the slug-like beast awake.

"I must be allowed to speak," Luke said softly. Bib echoed his words like a parrot.

"You weak-minded fool," Jabba hissed angrily. "He's using an old Jedi mind trick." He spat and pushed Bib away from him.

Luke stepped forward. "You will bring Captain Solo and the Wookiee to me."
Jabba simply laughed. "Your mind powers will not work on me, boy."
"Nevertheless, I am taking Captain Solo and his friends. You can either profit from this…or be destroyed."
Behind the throne, Threepio tried to wave his hand. "You're standing on a – "
"There will be no bargains!" Jabba interrupted.
Luke flicked his eyes to his right. There was Lando, still wearing his skiff disguise.
"I shall enjoy watching you die."
Luke reached out quickly, with his mind and hand. A blaster pistol from a nearby holster jumped into his palm and Luke swung his hand around to aim it at the slobbering gangster. Suddenly the floor dropped away from him and he was falling into the same pit that had claimed the dancer's life. A fat Gamorrean guard, caught too close to the edge of the pit, lost his balance and fell after him.

The hideous rancor beast, three times the height of Luke, scooped the guard up in one talloned hand and devoured him whole. Luke stared in horror, backing away as the Gamorrean's feet disappeared down the monster's gullet. This is it, Luke thought. I'm going to die…

He looked around quickly for somewhere to hide, saw a tiny cave where he might be able to avoid the beast's claws, and rolled into it. As the rancor advanced, he saw his chance. At the far side of the pit…a door! He dashed clear, under the beast's massive legs, and slammed his fist against the control panel. The door hissed open to reveal a grate…he was cornered. No way to escape and the beast coming straight for him!

Can you see a way for Luke to avoid certain death?

14 RETURN OF THE JEDI

Grabbing a skull off the floor, Luke hurled it at the control panel. The huge gate clattered down on the rancor's neck. The beast hit the dirt, gagging and choking for a second, and then it was dead. Luke sank back against the wall...he'd done it. He was still alive and the beast was dead.

The laughter above turned to anger.

"Bring me Solo and the Wookiee," Jabba bellowed. "They will all suffer for this!"

As Luke was dragged from the rancor's pit, he met Han Solo being marched from his cell. Threepio cast a shadow over the reunion, translating Jabba's words. "Oh dear. His high exaltedness Jabba has decreed that you are to be terminated, immediately."

"Good," Han said. "I hate long waits."

"You will be cast into the Pit of Carkoon, the nesting place of the all-powerful Sarlacc. In his belly you will find a new definition of pain and suffering as you are slowly digested over a thousand years..."

"You should have bargained, Jabba," Luke whispered. "This is the last mistake you'll ever make."

RETURN OF THE JEDI 15

Sand. Nothing but sand as far as the eye could see. Jabba's anti-gravity sail barges glided up to Sarlacc's mouth – a horrible pit ringed by thousands of razor-sharp teeth.

"I think my eyes are getting better," Han said quietly. "Instead of a big dark blur, I see a big light blur."

"Just stick close to Chewie and Lando, I've taken care of everything."

"Oh great…" Han didn't sound reassured.

A guard prodded Luke in the back with his spear. "Jabba," Luke called across the gap between the barges. "This is your last chance… free us or die."

"Put him in," Jabba ordered.

Luke saluted the sail barge, as if saying farewell. On the signal, Artoo launched Luke's lightsaber high into the air. Luke dropped, but instead of falling into the gaping mouth, he caught hold of the gangplank and used it as a springboard, somersaulting back over the guard's head. He reached out with his hand, summoning the lightsaber. His own lightsaber, not his father's. He cut through one…two…three…four guards with wide sweeps, sending one tumbling down to feed the Sarlacc. Moving quickly, he unshackled Han and Chewbacca.

nside the sail barge, Leia took advantage of the mayhem. She clambered on to the throne, hooked her chains around Jabba's throat and started to heave, pulling the chains tighter and tighter until they dug into the gangster's throat like a garrotte.

Which of Leia's chains will choke Jabba?

A
B
C
D

Leia yanked on the chains, pulling them deeper into Jabba's windpipe, choking him to death. With a last, dying effort, Jabba tensed every muscle and lurched forward. His eyes fluttered closed and he hit the floor, a dead weight.

Outside, the battle raged on.

Leia raced to Luke's aid as he parried stinging bolts of blaster fire. "Grab the gun," he yelled. "Point it at the deck!" The detonation rocked the barge, sending it to its destruction. Leia ran back down to Luke's side. He grabbed hold of a rope from the barge's rigging, took Leia under his arm and swung out on to the hovering escort barge. From here it was just a matter of getting the droids and getting out of there...

A squadron of TIE fighters escorted Emperor Palpatine's personal shuttle aboard the new Death Star. Ranks of stormtroopers, Darth Vader at their head, assembled in the docking bay to honour their ruler. The entrance to the shuttle came down and an old man emerged. Vader bowed in greeting before his wizened master.

"You have done well. And now I sense you wish to continue your search for young Skywalker. Patience...only together can we turn him to the dark side... It is all as I have foreseen." Palpatine cackled, the sound ringing through the hangar.

The *Millennium Falcon* and a smaller Rebel X-wing fighter flew out of Tatooine's atmosphere.

"Meet you back at the fleet," Luke promised.

"Sure, and Luke, I owe you one." Han's voice crackled. Luke smiled to himself, remembering his debts to Han. Behind him R2-D2 piped a question.

"Yes, Artoo, we're going to Dagobah. I have a promise to keep. To an old friend."

What co-ordinates should Luke set in the Astrogation system to reach the Dagobah System?

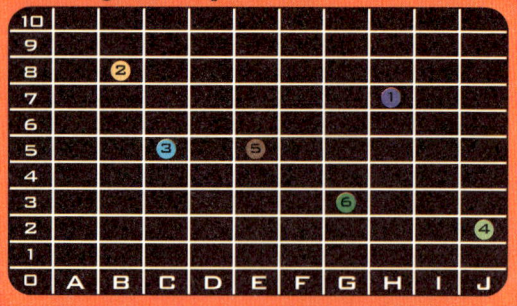

1 = Corellia
2 = Tatooine
3 = Hoth
4 = Dagobah System
5 = Coruscant
6 = Endor

Slowly skirting the swamp, Luke approached the dwelling. Crouching low, he entered. Yoda stood inside, smiling sadly. "That face you make...look I so old? When nine hundred years you reach, look as good you will not." The ancient Jedi Master climbed into bed. "Soon will I rest."
Luke sensed his meaning. "Master Yoda, you cannot die..."
"Strong I am in the Force, but not that strong. Twilight is upon me, and soon night must fall."
"But I need your help. I've come back to complete the training..." Luke appealed.
"No more training, already know what you need," Yoda sighed, sinking back into his pillow.
"Then I am a Jedi?" Luke questioned.

Yoda chuckled, the sound becoming a cough. "One thing remains." It was the one thing Luke feared most. "You must confront Vader. Then a Jedi you will be."

It was agonising to put the question into words, but he had to know. "Master Yoda…is Darth Vader my father?"

"Rest I need…" Yoda mumbled, rolling over.

"Yoda, I must know."

Silence. Then almost so quietly that he couldn't hear, "Your father he is…unfortunate that you rushed to face him, not ready for the burden were you. Remember, a Jedi's strength flows from the Force – put away anger, fear, aggression. When gone am I…last of the…Jedi you will be…pass on what you have learned…" Yoda's voice faded, death very close.

Decipher Yoda's last words:

THFRF…JS…BNPTHFR…SKYWBLKFR…

Clue: something has happened to the vowels in this slurred sentence.

"There…is…another…Skywalker…" The words faded.

Luke turned away, empty, and trudged slowly to his X-wing.

"I can't go on alone, Artoo."

"Yoda will always be with you," Obi-Wan Kenobi's image walked between the trees.

"Why didn't you tell me?" Luke pleaded, aching. "You told me Vader betrayed and murdered my father…"

"Your father was seduced by the dark side, Luke. He ceased to be Anakin Skywalker and became Darth Vader. I thought I could train him as a Jedi. I was wrong."

"There is still good in him," Luke insisted. "I can't kill my own father."

"Then the Emperor has already won," Obi-Wan said sadly. "You were our only hope."

"Yoda spoke of another," Luke pressed.

"Your twin sister. To protect you both from the Emperor, you were hidden from your father when you were born."

"Leia!" Luke gasped, suddenly understanding.

"Yes, but bury your feelings deep down, Luke. They could be twisted to serve the Emperor…"

The Rebel Starfleet gathered for a war council. Important information had fallen into Rebel hands at the cost of many lives – information on the Empire's newest battle station. "The Emperor has made a critical error," said Mon Mothma, leader of the Alliance, to the gathered room. Han was there, and Leia, Chewie, even Lando with his new title: General Calrissian. They watched her quietly and listened. "The time for our attack has come. We have the exact location of the Emperor's new Death Star. We also know that its weapons system is not yet operational."

A hologram flickered to life in the centre of the room, showing the Death Star orbiting a moon. "But most important, we have learned that the Emperor himself is overseeing the final stages of the operation…" The room fell quiet, absorbing her words, silently remembering the Bothans who had sacrificed their lives for this one chance to destroy the Empire.

RETURN OF THE JEDI 23

Admiral Ackbar stepped forward to speak. "Although incomplete, the Death Star is not defenceless. It is located by the forest moon of Endor, and protected by an energy shield." The hologram projected the image of a force shield around the space station. "No ships can fly through it. No weapons can penetrate it. The shield must be deactivated if any attack is to be attempted. General Calrissian has agreed to lead our fighters. General Madine," Ackbar handed over to Crix Madine, the man in charge of covert operations.

Madine spoke softly. "We have stolen an Imperial shuttle. Using a cracked code, a strike team will land on Endor and deactivate the shield generator."

Leia whistled between her teeth. "I wonder who they found to pull that off?"

"General Solo," Madine asked, "is your strike team assembled?" Leia gave Han the strangest of looks. Her shock and disbelief melted into admiration.

"The strike team's ready," Han said, grinning. "But I don't have a command crew for the shuttle."

At his side, Chewbacca growled that he was in.

Leia looked at Han. "Count me in, *General Solo*."

And from the door, Luke shouted, "I'm with you, too."

Can you pilot the path Lando will have to fly to lead the fighters to destroy the new Death Star?

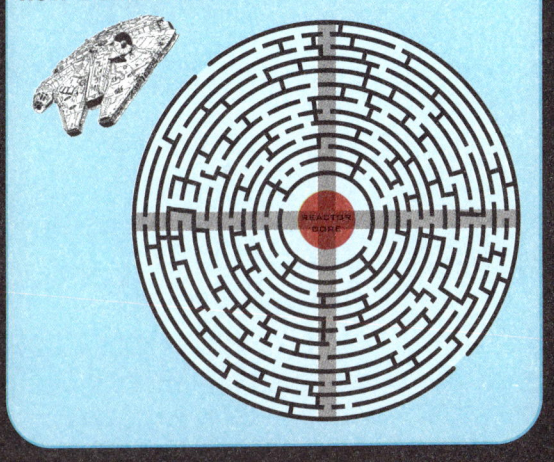

RETURN OF THE JEDI 25

he Imperial shuttle Tydirium decelerated from hyperspace, coming into range of a massive Imperial Star Destroyer.

"If they don't go for this, we're going to have to get out of here pretty quick." Han told the others what they already knew. This was make or break time.

"We have you on our screens," the voice of an Imperial Commander came over the comm system. "Please identify yourself."

"Shuttle Tydirium requesting deactivation of the deflector shields."

"Transmit the clearance code for shield passage."

Bothan spies have provided the code words "Lower Shield" and a key to electronic transmission.

The key is:
a=1   b=2   c=3   d=4

Can you work out the numbers Han needs to punch into the computer?

RETURN OF THE JEDI

Han transmitted the code.
"Now we find out if it's worth the price we paid," Leia said.
Then Luke spoke.
"Vader's on that ship...I can feel him..."
"Don't get jittery. It'll be okay. Chewie, let's keep our distance but not look like we're keeping our distance." Chewbacca grunted dubiously.
Finally the voice came back. "Shuttle Tydirium, deactivation of the shield will commence immediately. Follow your present course."
Han breathed a sigh of relief, and took them down to the moon.

The strike team approached the bunker on Endor, camouflaged by the dense forest. Han, Leia, Luke and Chewbacca led the troop, R2-D2 and C-3PO brought up the rear. They came to a ridge and crawled forwards on their bellies. Down below, two Imperial scouts had set up a temporary camp.
"Should we try and go around?"
"Nah, it'll take time. Chewie and I'll take care of this," Han said confidently.
"Quietly," Luke cautioned.

RETURN OF THE JEDI 27

Han flashed a bright smile and then he was off, sneaking down the side of the valley. They heard the twig snap and saw the scout slam his fist into Han's jaw. The other scout ran for his speeder bike. Chewie brought him down with his bowcaster before he had covered ten metres. "Great, just great..." Luke muttered. They raced down the slope to help, just in time to see two more scouts mount their bikes.

Leia leapt on to a free speeder bike, giving Luke time to leap on behind her before she started the engine.
Trees flashed by, the bike weaving through the thinnest of gaps. "Get alongside that one..." Luke yelled into her ear.
As the steering blades came close to locking, Luke leaped across the gap, hurling the scout from the driver's seat.
"Keep on that one, I'll take these two..." he shouted across, veering away in pursuit of the trailing pair.

28 RETURN OF THE JEDI

Leia chased the scout, but he was too good. Swerving, she tumbled to the floor, her bike flying into a tree. Leia hit the dirt and rolled, looking up to see the scout as he hit the stump of a fallen tree. She collapsed into darkness, leaving Luke alone to deal with remaining scouts.

Can you help Luke find a route to catch up with the Imperial scout?

START

Luke sent the first scout spinning into a tree, but in doing so was forced to jump free of his own bike. Standing quickly, he activated his lightsaber, and parried three shots from the rapidly approaching scout. Let the bike get close...closer, until it was on top of him...he brought the lightsaber slicing down through the speeder bike's steering blades. The bike span over and over in a crazy spiral, then burst into a ball of flames.

Luke deactivated the lightsaber and ran back through the forest to join the others.

"Where's Leia?" he called.

"I thought she was with you," Han said, clearly worried.

"You mean she didn't come back? We better go find her."

Darth Vader stepped through the doorway into the Emperor's observatory, his footsteps echoing coldly.

"I told you to remain on the command ship," Palpatine rasped.

Ignoring him, Vader stated simply, "A small Rebel force has penetrated the shield and landed on Endor. My son is with them."

"Are you sure?"

"I have felt him."

"Then you must go to the moon and wait for him."

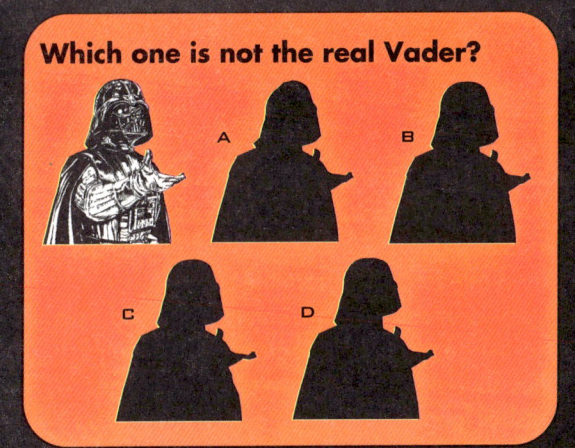

Which one is not the real Vader?

A B C D

Han and Luke stood beside Leia's wrecked bike.

"I'm afraid Artoo's sensors can find no trace of the princess," Threepio said. Only Chewbacca seemed uninterested in the clearing where Leia had come off her bike. He stood, sniffing, and then plunged into the forest.
"No wait, Chewie!" Luke called, chasing him, but it was too late. Chewbacca reached for the meat he'd found, and sprung the trap! A huge net lifted them all high into the air.

"Always thinking with your stomach," Han grumbled, upside down. They fell to the floor as Artoo released them from the net.
A crowd of small furry creatures emerged from the foliage to see what their trap had caught. They squeaked and squawked in a strange musical language, moving quickly to truss up their captives on carrying poles.

"My word, they seem to think I'm some kind of god," Threepio said, as the Ewoks carried him to their treetop village on a wooden throne. "And it seems you are to be the main course in a banquet in my honour."

The village buzzed with life as the Ewoks busied themselves making a fire beneath Han, Luke and Chewie.

Leia emerged from one of the treehouses, shaking her head. "Threepio, tell them they must be set free."

Han grinned. Luke smiled softly. Threepio jibbered at the Ewoks, but the fire building continued.

"Threepio," Luke called. "Tell them you'll become angry and use your magic." The Ewoks ignored him. As they were about to light the flames Luke gathered the Force and levitated Threepio's throne, making it fly above their heads.

In moments the Ewoks had cut them all free.

Later that night, Threepio told an animated tale of the Galactic War. Luke stopped listening and slipped outside.

"What's wrong?" Leia asked softly, taking his hand.

"Vader is here. I have felt him...I'm endangering the whole mission. I have to face him." It was hard to admit. "He's my father. There's more. If I don't make it back, you're the only hope for the Alliance."

"You have a power I could never have," she objected.

"You're wrong, Leia. You have that power too." Could he tell her? Should he? "The Force is strong in my family. My father has it, I have it...and my sister has it." He looked into her eyes. "It's you, Leia, you are my sister."

She was silent, then said softly, "I know. Somehow, I have always known…"

"Then you know why I have to face him. There is good in him, Leia. I can save him, I can turn him back to the good side. I have to try."

"**T**his is the Rebel that surrendered, Lord Vader."

"Good work. Search the forests and bring his companions to me," Vader hissed. "Now leave us."

They faced each other, father and son.

"The Emperor has been expecting you."

"I know, Father." It was a huge step for Luke, admitting the truth. "And I know there is good in you. Come with me, Father."

"You're wrong, my son. You don't know the power of the dark side. But soon the Emperor will show you."

he strike team arrived at the generator. One brave Ewok sneaked away and made off with a speeder bike. Three scouts gave chase, leaving only one to be distracted. Han, Leia and the others crept into the generator and began placing the charges – but were greeted by a squad of scout troopers hidden inside. They were escorted out at gunpoint, and surrounded by scout troopers and AT-STs.

Chief Chirpa sounded the attack. Rocks, tree stumps and vines brought down the scout walkers, as Han and Leia dashed back to the bunker door, and began trying to decode the lock.

Can you work out which three numbers they should have entered?

5, 7, 6, 9, 8, 12,

11, 16 ☐ ☐ ☐

RETURN OF THE JEDI

It didn't work. Han looked at it in disgust. "Well, I suppose I could try and hot-wire it..." he tugged doubtfully at the wires, splicing two together. There was a spark. "I think I got it," he called to Leia, who was crouching, giving him covering fire. "I got it!" But instead of opening, a second blast door closed over the entrance.

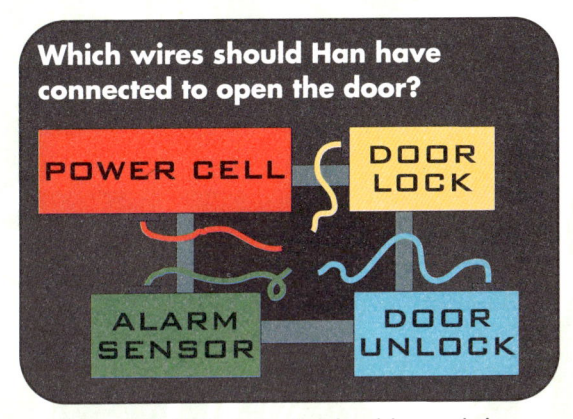

Which wires should Han have connected to open the door?

POWER CELL — DOOR LOCK
ALARM SENSOR — DOOR UNLOCK

A blaster bolt hit Leia in the shoulder and she cried out. Han crouched to check her wound. Behind him a voice barked, "Freeze – don't move!"

RETURN OF THE JEDI

Han looked at Leia. She secretly drew her blaster. "I love you," he mouthed.
"I know," she smiled, and shot the scout trooper – as a massive scout walker lumbered up.
Instead of shooting them, the hatch opened and Chewbacca stuck his head out.
Han grinned. "I got an idea."
He clambered into the captured scout walker. Soon, all the remaining troopers had been tricked out of the bunker.
"Let's go set those charges," he chuckled. Now it was up to the others.

In the Imperial throne room, Luke stood motionless, listening to the Emperor gloating. "Soon your friends will be dead, Skywalker. It was I who allowed the spies to steal the plans to my Death Star. My *fully operational* Death Star." He gave a vile cackle. "You want to strike me down? Good, I can feel your anger, give in to your hate. Strike me down and your journey towards the dark side will be complete!"
Luke's eyes darted from Vader to the Emperor, finally resting on his lightsaber.
"It's unavoidable. You, like your father, are mine!"
"No!" Luke cried out, summoning his lightsaber to hand and bringing the blade down in a scything sweep towards the Emperor's head. With dizzying speed Vader blocked the blow. The duel was incredible, blows arching high and low, one blade always met by the other. Luke ducked and kicked, sending Vader crashing down the stairs. Behind them, the Emperor cackled again. "Good. Your hate has made you strong."

RETURN OF THE JEDI

Suddenly, Luke stopped fighting, back-flipping up on to the overhead gangway. He turned off his lightsaber. "I will not fight you, Father. I sense the conflict in you. I don't believe you will kill me."

"There is no conflict!" Vader hissed, sending his lightsaber spinning and bringing the gangway down. Luke fell, rolling into the shadows to hide. "You cannot hide from me forever. Give yourself to the dark side. It is the only way you can save your friends… Your thoughts betray you… Your feelings for them are strong…especially your… sister… If you will not turn perhaps, she will."

"Nooooooo!" Luke screamed, hurtling from the shadows, hammering Vader back, blow after blow, beating him mercilessly. He sliced through Vader's right hand…his cybernetic right hand. Luke stopped fighting, gasping, and left Vader lying on the floor. This was the dark side.

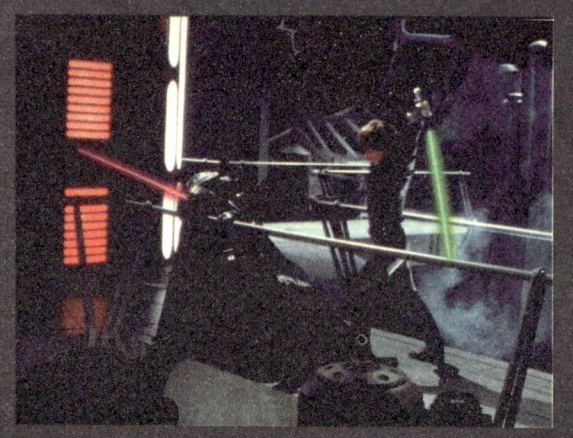

"Fulfill your destiny, take your father's place at my side!" the Emperor preened.

"Never," Luke said softly. "I'll never turn to the dark side. I am a Jedi, like my father before me."

"Then you will die," Palpatine hissed, raising his withered hands and unleashing waves of blue Force lightning from his fingers, the very essence of the dark side tearing through Luke's insides.

"Father, help me…" Luke cried out in agony. Vader looked from his son to the Emperor and back to his son. The goodness in him awoke. He reached out, grabbed the Emperor and staggered toward the chasm of the Death Star's power core. Bolts of lightning charged through Vader's body, but he didn't let go, condemning himself to death even as he saved his son's life. Vader hurled the Emperor's shrieking body into the black chasm and collapsed.

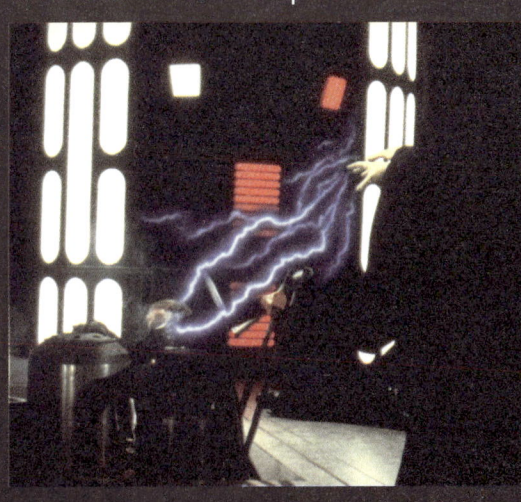

Luke dragged himself to his feet, and tried to haul his father through the doomed space station. They made it as far as the docking bay, stumbling towards one of the last remaining shuttles. The floor shook.
"Luke, help me take this mask off."
"But you'll die."
"Nothing can stop that now. Just once, let me look upon you with my own eyes." Luke helped him remove the black helmet. Beneath was a tired, dying old man. His father.
"Go my son, leave me," Anakin Skywalker whispered, his breath rapidly fading without the aid of the respirator.
"No, I've got to save you."
"You already have. You were right about me, Luke... Tell your sister...you...were...right..."
With that, Anakin Skywalker, Darth Vader, closed his eyes, and surrendered himself to death, redeemed.

"**T**he shield's down!" Ackbar crowed. Lando let out a relieved laugh. "I told you Han would have those deflectors down. Now let's blow this thing and go home." The *Millennium Falcon* homed in on the entrance to the central reactor core, leaving the other ships in the squadron to fight the space battle outside.

With TIE fighters on its tail, the *Millennium Falcon* cannot leave the Death Star by its entry route. Can you find another way away from the reactor core?

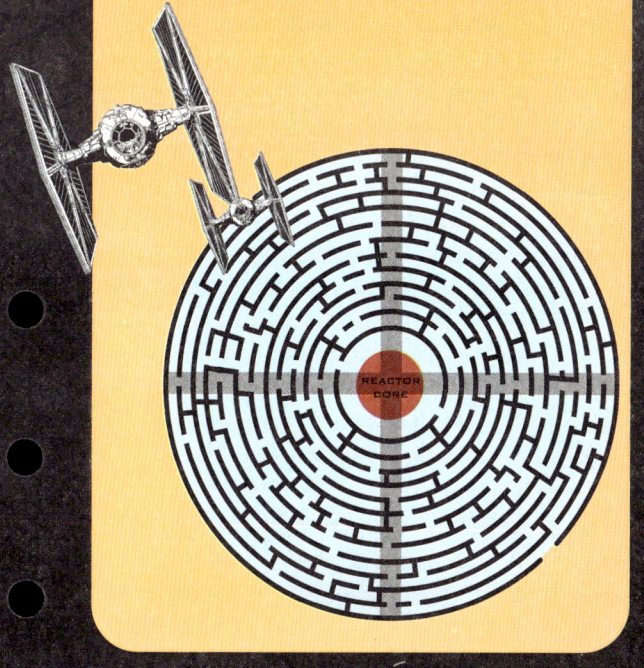

RETURN OF THE JEDI 43

"There's the superstructure," Lando called. "Watch for the main reactor shaft. This isn't going to be easy! Lock on to the strongest power source. Just pray it's the generator. Stay alert. We could run out of space real fast."

Behind the *Falcon*, an X-wing exploded, trying to fit through the narrowing shaft.

"Tight squeeze," Lando winced, as the *Falcon* clipped a pipe. "Okay – there it is!" He fired his torpedoes with a war cry and peeled off. "Direct hit!"

The ball of fire triggered a chain reaction of explosions that chased the *Falcon* out of the Death Star, with a fraction of a second to spare before the whole thing went up in flames.

On Endor, Leia and Han watched the explosions engulf the Death Star.

"I'm sure Luke wasn't on that thing," Han said quietly.

"He wasn't." Leia knew Luke was safe.

"You love him, don't you?" Han asked.

"Yes."

"Okay, fine. When he gets back...I won't get in the way."

Leia smiled ruefully. "It's not like that. He's my brother." Before Han had the chance to speak, she took his face in her hands and leaned in to kiss him.

That night Luke laid his father's armour out on a funeral pyre. He said his goodbyes to the man he never really knew.

The others were caught up in the celebration. The Emperor was dead. The Empire was dead! For a moment, gazing into the crackling fire, Luke thought he saw three images. Yoda. Ben...and was the third his father returned to the Force?

Leia touched his arm, and led him quietly back to the party...back to the warmth and love of his family.

Answers

page 2

page 5 C
page 7 4
page 8 C (Each shape has one more side than the previous shape.)
page 10

page 14 Luke must pick up a skull and throw it at the control panel, to close the gate on the Rancor.

46 RETURN OF THE JEDI

page 17 C
page 20 J2
page 21 There…is…another…Skywalker. (Each vowel has been changed to the letter following it in the alphabet.) 
page 25

page 26 12, 15, 23, 5, 18   19, 8, 9, 5, 12, 4 
page 29

RETURN OF THE JEDI   47

page 31 D
page 36

5, 7, 6, 9, 8, 12,

12, 11, 16 <u>15</u> <u>21</u> <u>20</u>

(To work out the numbers, follow the pattern +2-1+3-1+4-1 and so on.)

page 37

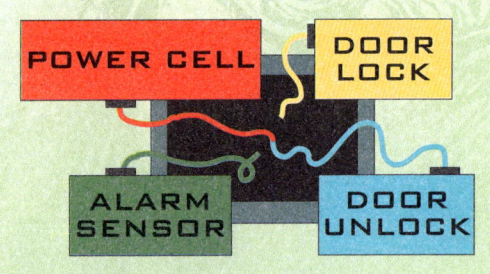

POWER CELL — DOOR LOCK
ALARM SENSOR — DOOR UNLOCK

page 43

48 RETURN OF THE JEDI